A MOTHER'S BOOK OF
BLESSINGS

A MOTHER'S BOOK OF
BLESSINGS

A TREASURY OF WISDOM FOR LIFE'S GREATEST MOMENTS

Edited by Natasha Tabori Fried and Lena Tabori
A Welcome Enterprises Book

NATIONAL
GEOGRAPHIC

WASHINGTON, D.C.

Since 1888, the National Geographic Society has funded more than 12,000 research, exploration, and preservation projects around the world. National Geographic Partners distributes a portion of the funds it receives from your purchase to National Geographic Society to support programs including the conservation of animals and their habitats.

National Geographic Partners
1145 17th Street NW
Washington, DC 20036-4688 USA

Get closer to National Geographic explorers and photographers, and connect with our global community. Join us today at nationalgeographic.com/join

For information about special discounts for bulk purchases, please contact National Geographic Books Special Sales: specialsales@natgeo.com

For rights or permissions inquiries, please contact National Geographic Books Subsidiary Rights: bookrights@natgeo.com

ISBN: 978-1-4262-1896-5

Designed by Kristen Sasamoto

Produced by Welcome Enterprises Inc.
6 West 18th Street, 4B, New York, N.Y. 10011
(212) 989-3200
www.welcomeenterprisesinc.com

Printed in China

17/RRDS/1

There is but one and only one,
Whose love will fail you never,
One who lives from sun to sun,
With constant fond endeavor.
There is but one and only one.
On Earth there is no other.
In heaven a noble work was done.
When God gave us a Mother.

—Old Irish verse

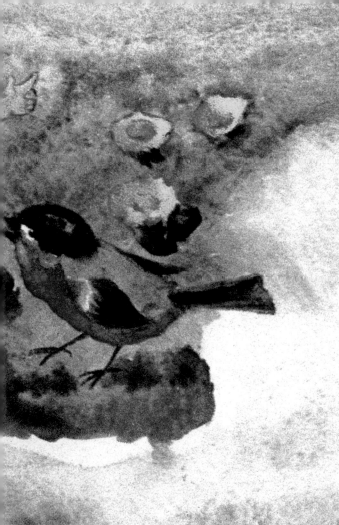

CONTENTS

INTRODUCTION

Blessed be.

When I started working on this book the first question I posed to myself was, "What is a blessing?" I looked it up. According to Merriam Webster it's the "act or words of one that blesses," "a thing conducive to happiness or welfare," or a "grace" said at a meal or occasion. That was pretty broad. I then asked a friend who was Catholic, who replied, "It's a prayer you say for someone else." Which prompted me to ask, "Then what is the difference between a blessing and a prayer?" Another friend offered this distinction: "A prayer is a conversation between you and God, but a blessing is a something you ask for on behalf of someone else." So, my spiritual but not terribly religious self arrived at the following definition: a blessing is like a wish, but a wish for someone else. In the context of this book, of course, blessings are wishes mothers offer their children throughout their lives, in moments both big and small: when they are born, when they get married, celebrate birthdays, head off to see the world, graduate, and so forth.

The more I thought about blessings, the more I found them everywhere: in the children's books I read to my son, from *Peter Pan* to *Winnie the Pooh* and *The Little Prince*; in the words of philosophers (Henry David Thoreau), great leaders (Mahatma Gandhi), sages (Buddha), spiritual teachers (Mother Teresa), authors (C. S. Lewis, Helen Keller), and poets (William Wordsworth, Maya Angelou). Sacred scriptures such as the Bible, the Torah, and the Quran were both inspiring and foundational.

Many blessings became personal to me:

· The Buddhist meditation my yoga teacher ends every class with, which appears in the Birthday section of this book.

· The quote from Mother Teresa that I keep on my office wall:
If you can't do it with love and cheerfulness, don't do it all—go home.

· The saying I sent out when my husband and I bought our house:
Life takes us to unexpected places…love brings us home.

· The framed piece of vintage art given to me by my sister reminding everyone:
The soul of this house is a friendly soul,
And it hails you—guest—with cheer,
Flings wide its doors with a welcome true
And opens its heart to you…
It offers rest and it bids you bide
Safe and snug by its fireside.

I've included a broad range of options—religious and secular, lighthearted rhymes and heartfelt prayers—so that you can choose what suits you best. The chapter on gratitude in its many forms might well be my favorite. For what more, in the end, could we as mothers hope for our children than for them to be blessed with gratitude? If they can remember, every day, to be thankful for who they are, whom they love, whom they are loved by, and the world around them—well then, they have everything.

—Natasha Tabori Fried

MOTHERHOOD

The moment a child is born, a mother is also born.
She never existed before.
The woman existed, but the mother, never.
A mother is something absolutely new.

—*Bhagwan Shree Rajneesh*

God's most precious work of art
Is the warmth and love
Of a mother's heart.

—*Irish blessing*

One generation plants the trees
Another gets the shade.

—*Chinese proverb*

Oh, what a power is motherhood,
Possessing a potent spell.
Love, Light, Blessings.

—*Euripides*

May God bless all the Mothers
That give of themselves
And tend to their household needs
Before the needs of self.
For they are there with comfort
For each child's broken heart,
Bringing them to God in prayer
With His love to impart.

—*Anonymous*

I remember my mother's prayers
And they have always followed me.
They have clung to me all my life.

—*Abraham Lincoln*

She is clothed with strength and dignity;
she can laugh at the days to come.
She speaks with wisdom and faithful
instruction is on her tongue.

—*Proverbs 31:25-26*

In heaven a noble work was done,
When God gave us a Mother.

—*Irish blessing*

Her children rise up and bless her.

—*Proverbs 31:28*

We give thanks for our maternal ancestors.
For those we never knew but who return to us
   in the faces of our sons and daughters.
For ancestors, with their strengths and frailties,
   who make us who we are.
For women who walked before us
   and worked the soil of our very lives.
For those who planted seeds, knowing the shade
   was for their children's children.
May we pass on to future generations
   the hope and promise revealed in their lives.

—*Lynn L. Caruso*

Now this is the day.
Our child,
Into the daylight
You will go standing.
Preparing for your day.

Our child, it is your day,
This day.
May your road be fulfilled.
In your thoughts may we live,
May we be the ones whom
   your thoughts will embrace,
May you help us all to finish our road.

—*Zuni Indian prayer*

A baby is a blessing.
A gift from heaven above,
A precious little angel
To cherish and to love.

—*Anonymous*

May the longtime sun shine
Upon you, all love surround you,
And the sweet light within you
Guide your way,

—*Irish blessing*

You are my sun, my moon and all of my stars.

—*e.e. cummings*

May your heart be happy
   and your days be bright.
May your roads be smooth
   and your burdens be light…
May you find the dreams
   and touch the stars and never
   forget how special you are.

      —Anonymous

Angels around us,
   angels beside us, angels within us.
Angels are watching over you
   when times are good or stressed.
Their wings wrap gently around you,
   whispering you are loved and blessed.

    —Anonymous

May the strength of the wind and the light of the sun,
The softness of the rain and the mystery of the moon
Reach you and fill you.
May beauty delight you and happiness uplift you,
May wonder fulfill you and love surround you.
May your step be steady and your arm be strong,
May your heart be peaceful and your word be true.
May you seek to learn, may you learn to live,
May you live to love, and may you love—always.

—*Celtic blessing*

Sun, Moon, Stars,
    all you that move in the heavens, hear us!
Into your midst has come a new life.
Make his/her path smooth, that he/she
    may reach the brow of the first hill!

Winds, Clouds, Rain, Mist,
    all you that move in the air, hear us!
Into your midst has come a new life.
Make his/her path smooth, that he/she
    may reach the brow of the second hill!

Hills, Valleys, Rivers, Lakes, Trees, Grasses,
    all you of the earth, hear us!
Into your midst has come a new life.
Make his/her path smooth, that he/she
    may reach the brow of the third hill!

Birds, great and small, that fly in the air,
Animals, great and small, that dwell in the forest,
Insects that creep among the grasses
   and burrow in the ground, hear us!
Into your midst has come a new life.
Make his/her path smooth, that he/she
   may reach the brow of the fourth hill!

All you of the heavens, all you of the air,
   all you of the earth, hear us!
Into your midst has come a new life.
Make his/her path smooth, then shall he/she
   travel beyond the four hills!

     —*Omaha Native American blessing*

Truly now,
Double thanks, triple thanks,
That we've been formed,
We've been given our mouths, our faces,
We speak, we listen, we wonder, we move,
Our knowledge is good,
We've understood what it is for,
We hear and we've seen
What is great and small,
Under the sky and on the earth.

—*Mayan blessing*

In every birth, blessed is the wonder.
In every creation, blessed is the new beginning.
In every child, blessed is life.
In every hope, blessed is the potential.
In every transition, blessed is the beginning.
In every existence, blessed are the possibilities.
In every love, blessed are the tears.
In every life, blessed is the love.
There are three names by which a person is called:
One which her father and mother call her,
And one which people call her,
And one which she earns for herself.
The best one of these
   is the one that she earns for herself.

—Jewish blessing

I am your parent; you are my child.
I am your quiet place, you are my wild.
I am your lullaby, you are my peekaboo.
I am your goodnight kiss, you are my I love you.

—*Maryann K. Cusimano*

When you were born,
   you cried and the world rejoiced.
Live your life in such a way that when you die,
   the world cries and you rejoice.

   —*Native American blessing*

May green be the grass you walk on,
May blue be the skies above you,
May pure be the joys that surround you,
May true be the hearts that love you.

—*Irish blessing*

MEALTIME

Round the table;
Peace and joy prevail.
May all who share
This season's delight
Enjoy countless more.

—*Chinese blessing*

Bless the food before us, the family beside us, and the love between us.

—*Anonymous*

Thank you for the wind, rain,
And sun and pleasant weather,
Thank you for this our food
And that we are together.

—*Mennonite blessing*

Food is symbolic of love when words are inadequate.

—*Alan D. Wolfelt*

Earth who gives to us this food,
Sun who makes it ripe and good,
Sun above and earth below,
Our loving thanks to you we show.
Blessings on our meal.

—*Secular blessing*

O Lord, bless the waters of the river.
Gladden the face of the earth.
May her furrows be watered, her fruits multiply;
Prepare it for seed and harvest.

—*Egyptian prayer*

Enough is a feast.

—*Dalai Lama*

Thank you for the world so sweet,
Thank you for the food we eat,
Thank you for the birds that sing,
Thank you, God, for everything.

—*Child's blessing*

Now that I am about to eat, O Great Spirit,
Let the feather of corn spring up in its time
And let it not wither but make full grains
For the fires of our cooking pots,
Now that I am about to eat.

—*Native American blessing*

Let us bless the source of life that brings forth bread from the earth.

—*Jewish blessing*

Be present at our table, Lord;
Be here, and everywhere adored;
Thy mercies bless and grant that we
May feast in fellowship with thee.

—*Christian prayer*

This ritual is One.
The food is One.
We who offer the food are One.
The fire of hunger is also One.
All action is One.
We who understand this are One.

—*Hindu blessing*

BEDTIME

Blessed art Thou, O Lord our God,
King of the Universe,
  who creates many living beings
  and the things they need.
For all that Thou hast created to sustain
  the life of every living being, blessed be
Thou, the Life of the Universe.

—*Jewish blessing*

Now I lay me down to sleep.
I pray thee Lord, my soul to keep.
See me safely through the night
  and wake me with the morning light.

—*Christian prayer*

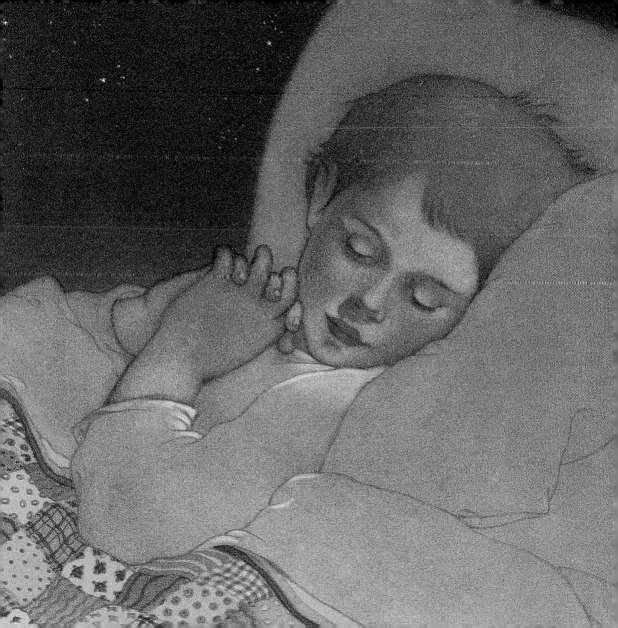

You know that place between sleep and awake, that place where you can still remember dreaming? That's where I will always love you, that's where I will be waiting.

—*J. M. Barrie*

The dark is dreaming, day is done.
Good night, good night, to everyone.
Good night to the birds, and the fish in the sea.
Good night to the bears, and good night to me.

—*Anonymous*

May all the blessings of our Lord touch your life today.
May He send His little angels to protect you on your way.
Such a miraculous gift, sent from above.
Someone so precious to cherish and love.
May sunshine and moonbeams dance over your head.
As you quietly slumber in your bed.
May good luck be with you wherever you go.
And your blessings outnumber the shamrocks that grow.

—*Irish blessing*

Lord, Keep us safe this night,
Secure from all our fears.
May angels guard us while we sleep,
Till morning light appears.

—*Baptist hymn by John Leland*

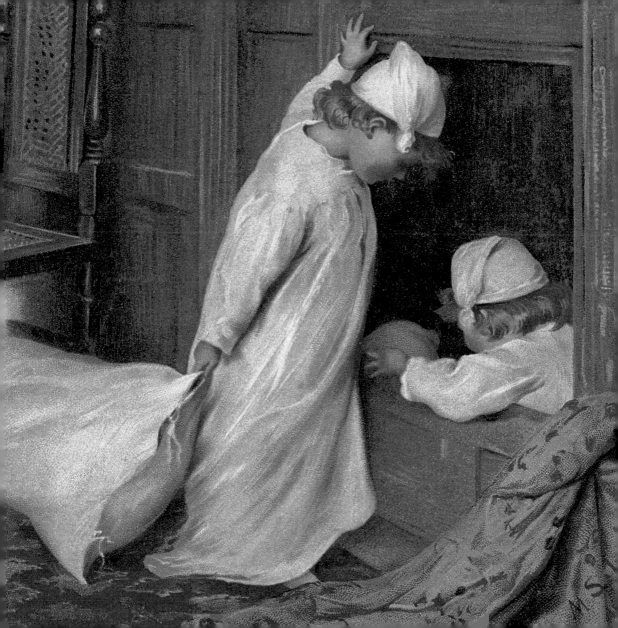

Now I lay me down to rest
Goddess, guard my little nest
Like the wee bird in the tree
Lovely Goddess, care for me.

—*Children's bedtime prayer*

I thank you, Lord, for knowing me
    better than I know myself, and for letting me
    know myself better than others know me.
Make me, I ask you then, better than they suppose.
And forgive me for what they do not know.

—*Muslim prayer*

That is perfect. This is perfect.
Perfect comes from perfect.
Take perfect from perfect,
The remainder is perfect.
May peace and peace and peace
  be everywhere.

—*Hindu Vedic prayer*

My God, I thank Thee, who hast made
The Earth so bright,
So full of splendor and of joy,
Beauty and light!
So many glorious things are here,
Noble and right!

—*Adelaide Anne Procter*

Wee Little One…
May you always walk in sunshine
May you never want for more.
May Irish angels rest their wings
  beside your nursery door.

—*Irish blessing*

Now the day is over
Night is drawing nigh,
Shadows of the evening
Steal across the sky.
Now the darkness gathers,
Stars begin to peep,
Birds and beasts and flowers
Soon will be asleep.
When the morning wakens,
Then may I arise,
Pure, and fresh, and sinless
In Thy Holy Eyes.

—Lutheran hymn,
  Rev. Sabine Baring-Gould

BIRTHDAYS

May love and laughter light your days
  and warm you heart and home,
May good and faithful friends
  be yours wherever you may roam,
May peace and plenty bless your world
  with joy that long endures,
May all life's passing seasons
Bring the best to you and yours.

—Irish blessing

Look to this day,
For its life,
The very life of life.
In its brief course lie all
The realities and verities of existence,
The bliss of growth,
The splendor of action,
The glory of power—

For yesterday is but a dream,
And tomorrow is only a vision,
But today, well lived,
Makes yesterday a dream of happiness
And every tomorrow a vision of hope.

—*Sanskrit proverb*

May there always be work for your hands to do,
May your purse always hold a coin or two,
May the sun always shine upon your window pane,
May a rainbow be certain to follow each rain,
May the hand of a friend always be near to you and
May your heart be full of cheer, gladness and love.

—*Anonymous*

The true way to live is to enjoy every moment
as it passes, and surely it is in the everyday things
around us that the beauty of life lies.

—*Laura Ingalls Wilder*

Life should not only be lived, it should be celebrated.

—*Rajneesh*

May the sun bring you new energy by day,
May the moon softly restore you by night,
May the rain wash away your worries,
May the wind blow new strength into your being,
May you walk gently through the world and know
   its beauty all the days of your life.

—Apache blessing

One of the best ways to worship God
Is simply to be happy.

—*Hindu saying*

On your birthday we pray
Green be the grass you walk on,
Blue be the skies above you,
Pure be the joys that surround you,
True be the hearts that love you.

—*Irish blessing*

Today will never come again.
Be a blessing.
Be a *friend*.
Encourage someone.
Take time to care.
Let your words heal, and not wound.

—*Anonymous*

Promise me you'll always remember:
You're braver than you believe, stronger than
you seem, and smarter than you think.

—Pooh's Grand Adventure

May you be
Safe and protected
May you be
Peaceful and happy
May you be
Healthy and at ease
Namaste
(from my heart to your soul)

　　—*A Buddhist meditation*
　　　　of loving kindness

Do all the good you can
By all the means you can,
In all the ways you can,
In all the places you can,
To all the people you can,
As long as ever you can.

—*John Wesley*

Today you are you, that's truer than true.
There is no-one alive who is Youer than You.

—*Dr. Seuss*

HOLIDAYS

Encircle this tree with your blessing.
May its twinkling lights remind us of
    the hope and promise of your coming.
May we find joy in the memories
    we share in its tinsel and trimmings.
May the presents we place beneath it
    give rise to an appreciation for
    the gift of your presence among us.
We ask this in your holy name.
Amen.

—*Christmas tree blessing*

May little chicks and flowers bring
Into your life the joys of Spring.

—*Easter blessing*

Black cats howling, witches prowling,
Fortunes told and futures seen.
Altogether spooks and weather
May it be a happy Halloween.

—*Halloween blessing*

Blessed are you, Lord, our God,
    sovereign of the universe who has kept us alive,
    sustained us, and enabled us to reach this season.

        —*Hanukkah blessing*

May this Diwali bring you the utmost
   in peace and prosperity.
May lights triumph over darkness.
May peace transcend the earth.
May the spirit of light illuminate the world.
May the lights that we lit at Diwali show us
   the way and lead us together on the path
   of peace and social harmony.

   —*Diwali blessing*

We return thanks to our mother, the Earth,
   which sustains us.
We return thanks to the rivers and streams,
   which supply us with water.
We return thanks to all herbs,
   which furnish medicines for the cure of our diseases.
We return thanks to the moon and stars,
   which have given to us their light when the sun was gone.
We return thanks to the sun,
   which has looked upon the Earth with a beneficent eye.
Lastly, we return thanks to the Great Spirit,
   in Whom is embodied all goodness,
   and Who directs all things for the good of Her children.

   —*Iroquois thanksgiving prayer*

At New Year and always, may peace and love fill your heart, beauty fill your world, and contentment and joy fill your days.

—*Chinese New Year's blessing*

And now we welcome the new year,
full of things that have never been.

—*Rainer Maria Rilke*

May the spirit of Christmas bring you peace,
The gladness of Christmas give you hope,
The warmth of Christmas grant you love.

—Christmas blessing

The holiest of all holidays are those
Kept by ourselves in silence and apart;
The secret anniversaries of the heart,
When the full river of feeling overflows;—
The happy days unclouded to their close;
The sudden joys that out of darkness start
As flames from ashes; swift desires that dart
Like swallows singing down each wind that blows!
White as the gleam of a receding sail,
White as a cloud that floats and fades in air,
White as the whitest lily on a stream,
These tender memories are;—a fairy tale
Of some enchanted land we know not where,
But lovely as a landscape in a dream.

—*Henry Wadsworth Longfellow*

For each new morning with its light,
For rest and shelter of the night,
For health and food,
For love and friends,
For everything
Thy goodness sends.

For flowers that bloom about our feet;
For tender grass, so fresh, so sweet;
For song of bird, and hum of bee;
For all things fair we hear or see,
Father in heaven, we thank Thee!

—*Ralph Waldo Emerson,*
    Thanksgiving prayer

We shall find peace. We shall hear the angels.
We shall see the sky sparkling with diamonds.

—*Anton Chekhov*

The light of the Christmas star to you,
The warmth of home and hearth to you,
The cheer and good will of friends to you,
The hope of a childlike heart to you,
The joy of a thousand angels to you,
The love of the Son,
And God's peace to you.

—*Irish blessing*

TRAVEL

To move, to breathe, to fly, to float,
To gain all while you give,
To roam the roads of lands remote,
To travel is to live.

—*Hans Christian Andersen*

There are far better things ahead than any we leave behind.

—*C. S. Lewis*

If adventures will not befall a young lady
in her own village, she must seek them abroad.

—*Jane Austen*

As you walk and eat and travel, be where you are.
Otherwise you will miss most of your life.

—*Buddha*

May it be Your will, o Lord, our God
   and the God of our ancestors,
   that You lead us toward peace,
   guide our footsteps toward peace,
   and make us reach our desired destination
   for life, gladness, and peace.
May You rescue us from the hand of every foe,
   ambush along the way, and from all manner
   of punishments that assemble to come to earth.
May You send blessing in our handiwork,
   and grant us grace, kindness, and mercy
   in Your eyes and in the eyes of all who see us.

                —*Jewish wayfarer's prayer*

If I rise on the wings of the dawn,
if I settle on the far side of the sea,
even there Your hand will guide me.

—*Psalm 139*

May the road rise to meet you,
May the wind be at your back,
May the sun shine warm upon your face.
May the rain fall softly on your fields,
And until we meet again,
May God hold you in the palm of His hand.

—*Irish blessing*

May angels fly with you wherever you roam
And guide you back safely to family and home!

—*Anonymous*

Keep your eyes on the stars and your feet on the ground.

—*Theodore Roosevelt*

May your joys be as deep as the oceans,
Your troubles as light as its foam,
And may you find sweet peace of mind
Wherever you may roam.

   —Irish blessing

NATURE

Hurt no living thing;
Ladybird, nor butterfly,
Nor moth with dusty wing,
Nor cricket chirping cheerily,
Nor grasshopper so light of leap,
Nor dancing gnat, nor beetle fat,
Nor harmless worms that creep.

—*Christina Rossetti*

The kiss of the sun for pardon,
The song of the birds for mirth—
One is nearer God's heart in a garden
Than anywhere else on earth.

—*Dorothy Frances Gurney*

Little drops of water,
Little grains of sand.
Make the mighty ocean,
And the pleasant land.

Thus the little minutes,
Humble though they be,
Make the mighty ages
Of eternity.

Little deeds of kindness,
Little words of love,
Make this earth an Eden
Like heaven above.

—*Isaac Watts*

Give me the splendid silent sun
    with all his beams full-dazzling,
Give me autumnal fruit ripe
    and red from the orchard,
Give me a field where
    the unmow'd grass grows,
Give me an arbor,
    give me the trellis'd grape,
Give me fresh corn and wheat,
    give me serene-moving animals
    teaching content,
Give me nights perfectly quiet as on
    high plateaus west of the Mississippi,
    and I looking up at the stars,
Give me odorous at sunrise
    a garden of beautiful flowers
    where I can walk undisturb'd.

—*Walt Whitman*

If you would be happy all your life, plant a garden.

—*Anonymous*

And the wind said,
May you be as strong as the oak,
  yet flexible as the birch.
May you stand as tall as the redwood,
  live gracefully as the willow
  and may you always bear fruit
  all your days on this earth.

  —*Native American blessing*

Plant four rows of squash:
Squash gossip
Squash indifference
Squash grumbling
Squash selfishness

Plant four rows of lettuce:
Lettuce be faithful
Lettuce be kind
Lettuce be obedient
Lettuce really love one another

Water freely with patience and
Cultivate with love.
There is much fruit in your garden
Because you reap what you sow.

—*Anonymous*

Love all Creation,
The whole of it and every grain of sand.
Love every leaf,
Every ray of God's light.
Love the animals,
Love the plants,
Love everything.
If you love everything,
You will perceive
The divine mystery in things.
And once you have perceived it,
You will begin to comprehend it ceaselessly,
More and more everyday.
And you will at last come to love the whole world
With an abiding universal love.

—*Fyodor Dostoyevsky*

All things bright and beautiful,
   All creatures, great and small,
All things wise and wonderful,
   The Lord God made them all.

Each little flower that opens,
   Each little birth that sings,
He made their glowing colors,
   He made their tiny wings;

The rich man in his castle,
   The poor man at his gate,
God made them, high or lowly,
   And ordered their estate.

The purple-headed mountain,
  The river running by,
The sunset and the morning,
  That brightens up the sky,

The cold wind in the winter,
  The pleasant summer sun,
The ripe fruits in the garden—
  He made them every one.

—*Cecil Frances Alexander*

Watch with glittery eyes the whole world
around you, because the greatest secrets
are always hidden in the most unlikely places.

—*Roald Dahl*

GRADUATION

Give strength, give thought,
  give deeds, give wealth;
Give love, give tears, and give thyself.
Give, give, be always giving;
Who gives not is not living.
The more you give, the more you live.

—*Anonymous*

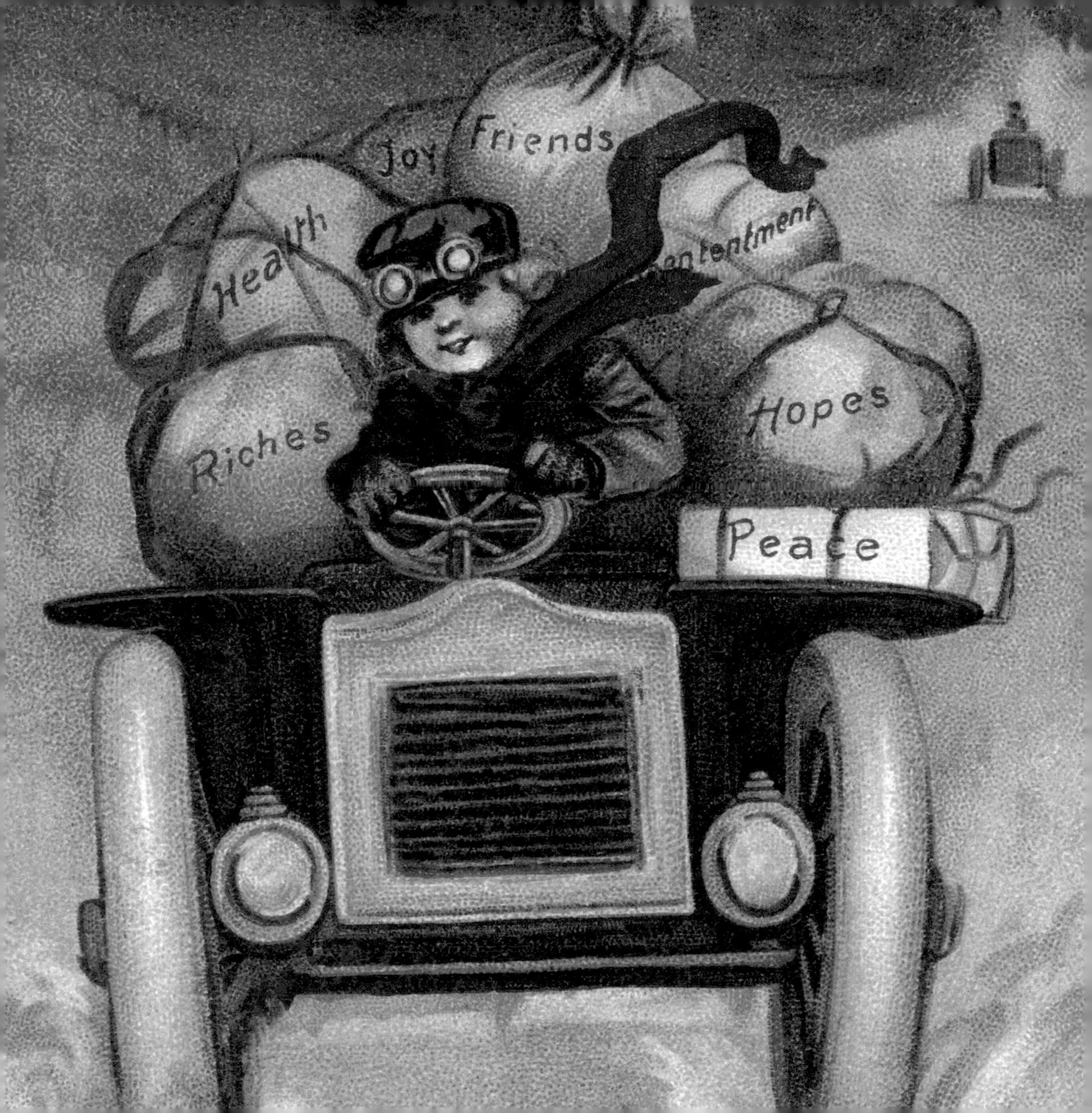
Joy
Friends
Health
Contentment
Riches
Hopes
Peace

Do not seek too much fame,
But do not seek obscurity.
Be proud.
But do not remind the world
  of your deeds.
Excel when you must,
But do not excel the world.
Many heroes are not yet born,
Many have already died.
To be alive to hear this song
  is a victory.

—*West African song*

The thought manifests as the word;
The word manifests as the deed;
The deed develops into habit;
And habit hardens into character.
So watch the thought and its way with care,
And let it spring from love
Born out of concern for all beings.

—*Buddha*

This is your life, not someone else's. It is your own feeling of what is important, not what people will say…

The important thing is to be sure that those who love you, whether family or friends, understand as nearly as you can make them understand. If they believe in you, they will trust your motives. But do not ask or expect to have anyone with you on everything. Do not try for it. To reach such a state of unanimity would mean that you would risk losing your own individuality to attain it…

—*Eleanor Roosevelt*

There's the whole world at your feet.

—Mary Poppins

If you have built castles in the air, your work
need not be lost; that is where they should be.
Now put the foundations under them.

—*Henry David Thoreau*

The simplest acts of kindness
are by far more powerful than
a thousand heads bowing in prayer.

—*Mahatma Gandhi*

Wherever you go, go with all your heart.

—*Confucius*

Be who you are and may you be blessed in all that you are.

—*Jewish blessing*

Go forth and set the world on fire.

—*St. Ignatius of Loyola*

If you can't do it with love and cheerfulness, don't do it at all—go home.

—*Mother Teresa*

There will come a time when you believe
everything is finished. That will be the beginning.

—*Louis L'Amour*

WEDDING

Happy is the bride that rain falls on.
May your mornings bring joy
and your evenings bring peace.
May your troubles grow few as your
blessings increase.
May the saddest day of your future
Be no worse than the happiest day
of your past.
May your hands be forever clasped
in friendship
And your hearts joined forever in love.

—Irish blessing

When two people are at one in their innermost hearts,
They shatter even the strength of iron or of bronze.
And when two people understand each other in their inmost hearts,
Their words are sweet and strong like the fragrance of orchids.

—*I Ching*

Divine love is a sacred flower,
which in its early bud is happiness,
and in its full bloom is heaven.

—*Eleanora Louisa Hervey*

May the blessing of God rest upon you,
May His peace abide within you,
May His presence illuminate your heart,
Now and forevermore.

—*Sufi blessing*

May love and laughter light your days
    and warm your heart and home,
May good and faithful friends be yours
    wherever you may roam,
May peace and plenty bless your world
    with joy that long endures,
May all life's passing seasons bring the best
    to you and yours.

—*Irish blessing*

Love does not consist in gazing
at each other, but in looking outward
together in the same direction.

—*Antoine de Saint-Exupéry*

As the sun illuminates the moon and stars,
So let us illumine one another.

—*Anonymous*

Time is
Too slow for those who Wait,
Too swift for those who Fear,
Too long for those who Grieve,
Too short for those who Rejoice,
But for those who Love,
Time is not.

—*Henry van Dyke*

Bless them as unmoving and eternal
May their lives flourish like luxuriant trees.
May they, bride and groom, together with heaven and earth,
With the sun and the moon, continue to give out light and radiance.

Japanese wedding blessing

The great secret of a successful marriage is to treat
all disasters as incidents and no incident as a disaster.

—*Sir Harold Nicolson*

Let there be spaces in your togetherness.

— *Kahlil Gibran*

Love is patient, love is kind.
It does not envy, it does not boast,
 it is not proud.
It is not rude, it is not self-seeking,
 it is not easily angered,
 it keeps no record of wrongs.
Love does not delight in evil
 but rejoices with the truth.
It always protects, always trusts,
 always hopes, always perseveres.

Love never fails.
But where there are prophecies,
  they will cease; where there are
  tongues, they will be stilled;
  where there is knowledge,
  it will pass away....
And now these three remain:
  faith, hope and love.
But the greatest of these is love.

  —1 Corinthians 13:4-8, 13

Many waters cannot quench love,
   neither can floods drown it.
If a man offered for love all the wealth
   of his house, he would be utterly despised.

—*Song of Solomon 8:7*

May your life be filled with laughter.
May your heart be filled with song.
May your eyes be filled with beauty.
May your soul always know to whom
  you belong.

—*Irish blessing*

The things that we love tell us what we are.
—*Thomas Aquinas*

Now you will feel no rain,
For each of you will be shelter to the other.
Now you will feel no cold,
For each of you will be warmth to the other.
Now there is no more loneliness.
Now you are two persons,
But there is only one life before you.
Go now to your dwelling place,
To enter into the days of your togetherness,
And may your days be good and long upon this earth.

—Native American wedding prayer

HOUSEWARMING

Bless our home as we come and go.
Bless our home as our children grow.
Bless our families as they gather in;
Bless our home with love and friends.

For each new morning with its light,
For rest and shelter of the night,
For health and food, for love of friends,
For everything thy goodness sends.

—*Ralph Waldo Emerson*

May its windows catch the sun and its doors be open wide to friends and loved ones. May each room resound with laughter and may the walls shut out troubles and hold in warmth and cheer. May this house be filled with joy in the morning and sweet dreams at night. May it be a home where love has come to live.

—*Anonymous*

A home is built with peace and love,
and not of wood or stone, a place where
happiness lives, and memories are sown.

—*Anonymous*

Let no sadness come through this gate.
Let no trouble come to this dwelling.
Let no fear come through this door.
Let no conflict be in this place.
Let this home be filled with the blessing
   of joy and peace.

   —*Jewish blessing*

May the roof above us never fall in,
And may we friends gathered below
    never fall out.

—*Irish blessing*

The most important work you will ever do
will be within the walls of your own home.

—*Harold B. Lee*

Home is the place where,
when you have to go there,
they have to take you in.

—*Robert Frost*

Home is a place where we can be silent and still be heard. Where we can ask and find out who we are. Where sorrow is divided and joy multiplied. Where we share and love and grow.

—*Anonymous*

If there is righteousness in the heart,
There will be beauty in the character.
If there is beauty in the character,
There will be harmony in the home.
If there is harmony in the home,
There will be order in the nation.
If there is order in the nation,
There will be peace in the world…

—*Chinese blessing*

The ache for home lives in all of us, the safe place where we can go as we are and not be questioned.

—*Maya Angelou*

May the warm winds of Heaven
   blow softly on your home,
And the great Spirit bless all
   who enter there.
May your moccasins make
   happy tracks in many snows,
And may the rainbow always
   touch your shoulder.

   —*Cherokee blessing*

GRATITUDE

To everything there is a season,
  and a time to every purpose under heaven:
A time to be born, and a time to die;
  a time to plant, and a time to pluck up
  that which is planted;
A time to kill, and a time to heal;
  a time to break down, and a time to build up;
A time to weep, and a time to laugh;
  a time to mourn, and a time to dance…
A time to rend, and a time to sew;
  a time to keep long silence, and a time to speak;
A time to love, and a time to hate;
  a time of war, and a time of peace.

—*Ecclesiastes 3:1-4, 7-8*

Dear God, hear and bless
Your beasts and singing birds;
And guard with tenderness
Small things that have no words.

—*Anonymous*

Gratitude unlocks the fullness of life.
It turns what we have into enough, and more.
It turns denial into acceptance, chaos to order,
confusion to clarity.

—*Melody Beattie*

Treat the Earth and all that dwell thereon with respect.
Remain close to the Great Spirit.
Show great respect for your fellow beings.
Work together for the benefit of all Mankind.
Give assistance and kindness wherever needed.
Do what you know to be right.
Look after the well being of mind and body.
Dedicate a share of your efforts to the greater good.
Be truthful and honest at all times.
Take full responsibility for your actions.

—Native American Ten Commandments

Always remember to forget the things that made you sad.
But never forget to remember the things that made you glad.
Always remember to forget the friends that proved untrue.
But never forget to remember those that stuck by you.
Always remember to forget the troubles that passed away.
But never forget to remember the blessings that come each day.

—*Irish blessing*

Gratitude takes three forms:
A feeling in the heart, an expression
in words, and a giving in return.

—*Arabic proverb*

Life takes us to unexpected places…love brings us home.

—*Anonymous*

May God give you…
For every storm, a rainbow,
For every tear, a smile,
For every care, a promise,
And a blessing in each trial.
For every problem life sends,
  a faithful friend to share.
For every sigh, a sweet song.
And an answer for every prayer.

—*Irish blessing*

May my feet rest firmly on the ground
May my head touch the sky
May I see clearly
May I have the capacity to listen
May I be free to touch
May my words be true
May my heart and mind be open
May my hands be empty to fill the need
May my arms be open to others
May my gifts be revealed to me
So I may return that which has been given
Completing the great circle.

—*Guru Rinpoche*

Let us be grateful to people
who make us happy;
They are the charming gardeners
who make our souls blossom.

—*Marcel Proust*

Though nothing can bring back
The hour of splendor in the grass,
Of glory in the flower;
We will grieve not,
Rather find strength
In what remains behind.

—*William Wordsworth*

Hold on to what is good
   even if it is a handful of earth.
Hold on to what you believe
   even if it is a tree that stands by itself.
Hold on to what you must do
   even if it is a long way from here.
Hold on to life even when
   it is easier letting go.
Hold on to my hand even when
   I have gone away from you.

            —*Pueblo verse*

Some people grumble that roses have thorns;
I am grateful that thorns have roses.

—*Jean-Baptiste Alphonse Karr*

ACKNOWLEDGMENTS

The editors wish to thank and to acknowledge the tremendous gifts of our Welcome designer, Kristen Sasamoto, who sifted through thousands of images to find those that grace this book, whose aesthetic gifts are unparalleled, and whose patience is limitless. She is truly our partner in this venture.

At National Geographic, our gratitude goes to: Bill O'Donnell, Director of Retail & Special Sales, without whom we would never have met Lisa Thomas, Publisher & Editorial Director, and Hilary Black, Deputy Editor, whose idea this was. Allyson Johnson, Editorial Project Manager, whose decency, good will, and talent have been indispensible. Patrick Bagley, Photo Editor, whose kindness was gratefully received. And Meka Owens who, with a laugh, made certain everything got where it needed to go.

ILLUSTRATIONS CREDITS

Anne Anderson (147); Mary Anderson (136); Eulalie Banks (134-135); Sybil Barham (230-231, 256-257); Enoch Bolles (286); Augusta Briggs (241); C. M. Bura (88, 139); D. Burton (278-279); Ruth Cobb (298); Pauli Ebner (329); Maginel Wright Enright (148, 175); Hazel Frazee (246); Charles H. Freeman (55); Ruth Mary Hallock (211); Frank Hart (184); Will Hollingsworth (71); Frances Tipton Hunter (120-121, 128, 144); Phil Lyford (280); Edna Merritt (24, 220-221, 228, 351); G. Meschini (290-291); Sibylle von Olfers (208, 301); Ethel Parkinson (140); Maxfield Parrish (268); Susan Beatrice Pearse (56); M. A. Peart (297); Fern Bisel Peat (90); Hannes Petersen (289); Maud & Miska Petersham (1, 311, 352); Margaret Evans Price (42, 94); Frederick Winthrop Ramsdell (18); E. Dorothy Rees (127); Jessie Willcox Smith (13, 28, 37, 40-41, 50, 72-73, 78, 158, 215, 218, 224, 234, 262, 332-333, 336); Gustaf Tenggren (116, 172, 250); Roger Vernam (60, 84, 165); Edward A. Wilson (182-183); Blanche Fisher Wright (87)

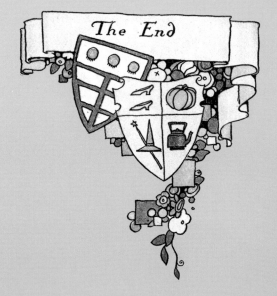

The End